To:

....

From:

....

Other books in this series

◆

Mother's Love

Love You, Dad

True Love

Friends Forever

The World Awaits

The Little Book of Thanks

Amazing Moms

The Wisdom of Moms

amazing dads

Love *and* Lessons *From the* Animal Kingdom

Bridget E. Hamilton

NATIONAL GEOGRAPHIC

Washington, D.C.

Since 1888, the National Geographic Society has funded more than 12,000 research, exploration, and preservation projects around the world. National Geographic Partners distributes a portion of the funds it receives from your purchase to National Geographic Society to support programs including the conservation of animals and their habitats.

National Geographic Partners
1145 17th Street NW
Washington, DC 20036-4688 USA

Become a member of National Geographic and activate
your benefits today at natgeo.com/jointoday.

For information about special discounts for bulk purchases, please contact
National Geographic Books Special Sales: specialsales@natgeo.com

For rights or permissions inquiries, please contact National Geographic
Books Subsidiary Rights: bookrights@natgeo.com

ISBN: 978-1-4262-1808-8

Interior design by Nicole Miller

Printed in Hong Kong

17/THK/1

To my amazing dad,
thanks for everything.

◆

Introduction

There is that one special person who is always your biggest fan, your most tireless coach, and your friend no matter what: your dad. In the animal kingdom, dads don't often stand out in the role of parent, mentor, or friend. But some are doing their part to change that reputation. A male raccoon dog, for example, does an amazing job providing for his pups alongside their mom. He teaches them the skills they'll need outside the safety of the den, such as how to find prey and defend themselves. It's his valuable lessons and seasoned patience that prepare them for the road ahead. Animal dads make extraordinary sacrifices for their children, but, like human dads, they usually don't take credit for their children's success. They know when it's your time to shine and take on the world.

Raccoon dogs are members of the wolf family found in Asia and Europe. Despite the striking similarity, they are not closely related to raccoons.

"Happy are those who **dare courageously** to defend what they love."

◆

—Ovid

A father golden tamarin will introduce solid food into his children's diet by feeding them mashed bananas.

"Children have never been very good at listening to their elders, **but they have never failed to imitate them.**"

◆

—JAMES BALDWIN

Male deer grow new antlers annually because the old ones fall off naturally every winter.

Ruler of the Roost

Emperor penguins live up to their name, as they rule the Antarctic roost. While Mom goes off on a months-long search for food to share with their unhatched chick, Dad stays with the newly laid egg. He must keep it warm by cradling it on his feet and covering it with his brood pouch, a layer of feathered skin used just for this purpose. For the next two months this is his only job and he will forsake everything else, including eating, relying on his own fat reserves to see him through. If their chick hatches before Mom returns, Dad will feed him, but once Mom is back both share responsibility for raising and feeding the chick. The chick eventually develops feathers and is able to survive outside his parents' brood pouches. Soon they will all return to the sea, their true home.

Unlike other birds, male emperor penguins do not sit on their eggs; they stand, balancing the egg on their feet.

*Puppies need to consume twice as much protein
as adult dogs for healthy growth.*

"It is vital [when] educating our children's brains that **we do not neglect to educate their hearts.**"

◆

—THE DALAI LAMA

"If there ever comes a day when we can't be together, **keep me in your heart.** I'll stay there forever."

◆

—A. A. Milne

Bison are born with reddish fur. They do not turn completely brown until around four months.

There From Day One

From the very beginning, common marmoset dads are there to help. After assisting as a midwife during the babies' birth and licking them clean, Dad is ready for his turn, carrying the little ones as they ride on his back for the first two weeks of their lives. The babies depend on their father to be their caregiver during those early days, and he is known to respond within 45 seconds of hearing their cries. Mom continues to feed the babies during that time but relies on Dad for a lot of help. Common marmosets are very small, so the enormous task of caring for young, often twins, must be shared between parents. Within a few weeks the babies are out exploring, but need Mom and Dad's help as they learn to take care of themselves.

Common marmosets are very communicative with one another and are known to wait for another monkey to stop talking before they respond.

Bald eagles share equally in parenting duties, from building the nest to feeding the hatchlings. The same breeding pair will return to their nesting site for as many as 35 years.

Eagle nests are called aeries. At least one parent is present at all times to warm the eggs and ward off thieving squirrels, ravens, and gulls.

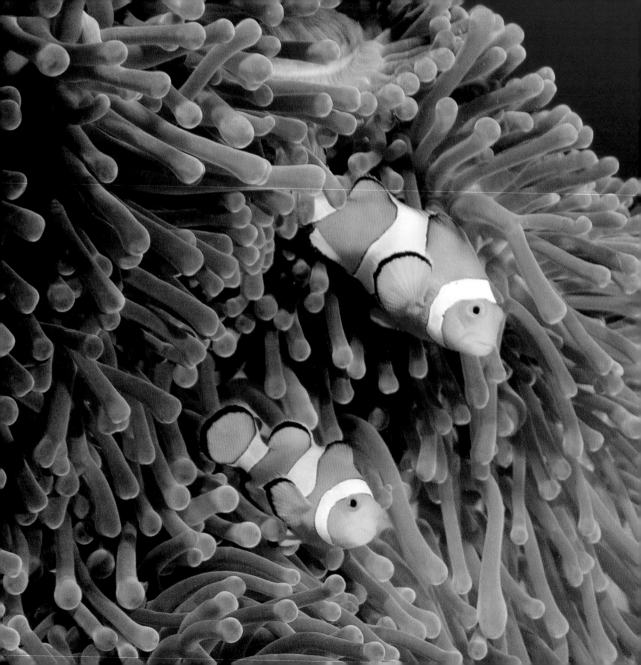

"Other things may change us, but we start and end **with the family.**"

◆

—ANTHONY BRANDT

The male clownfish will meticulously clean an anemone to use as a nursery and is solely responsible for the eggs.

Protector in Chief

A sea lion father knows the importance of claiming territory; in fact, once he establishes a rookery he normally rules the area for up to two years. These dads have the macho looks to back up the claim—male Steller sea lions, the largest seals in the family Otariidae, can weigh up to 1,543 pounds (700 kg). Between May and July every year, Dad's home will become overrun with pups, and he needs to provide a safe place for them. Pups take to the water quickly and begin swimming four to six weeks after they are born. Mom might be the one that provides the nutrition and attention a pup needs to develop, but Dad is busy maintaining the rookery and keeping everyone safe from harm.

Sea lions are social throughout the year and are often seen together along the coast in groups ranging from dozens to hundreds.

Most big cats are solitary, but lions live in social prides. The alpha male is the protector and the cubs learn by mimicking their father's behavior.

Lions show affection by nuzzling, licking, and play-fighting with their cubs.

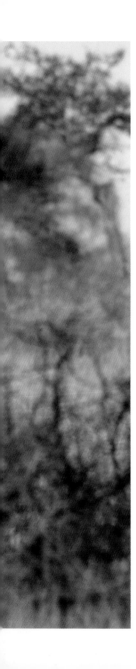

"**Day by day nothing seems to change,** but pretty soon everything is different."

◆

—BILL WATTERSON

Three to four weeks after birth, giraffes are gathered into "nurseries,"
where they play and learn necessary life skills together.

Homebody

Living along the water's edge in the tropical paradise of Panama, it's good to know how to build a snug home. Male northern jacanas have got that down pat. They build platform-style nests, and each male is the main caretaker of up to four eggs. While the eggs are incubating, Dad will continue to improve the nest for the chicks' arrival, adding more comforting material from nearby plants. The eggs hatch 28 days later, and that's when Dad's job really begins. Female jacanas will defend the territory surrounding the nests, but Dad is responsible for raising the chicks. Chicks don't spend much time in their nicely prepared nest—only about 24 hours—at which point the males will lead them into the outside world. Within eight weeks the chicks grow more independent, but they stay close to Dad for about a year before heading out on their own.

A male jacana will sing a group of notes when his chicks are near.

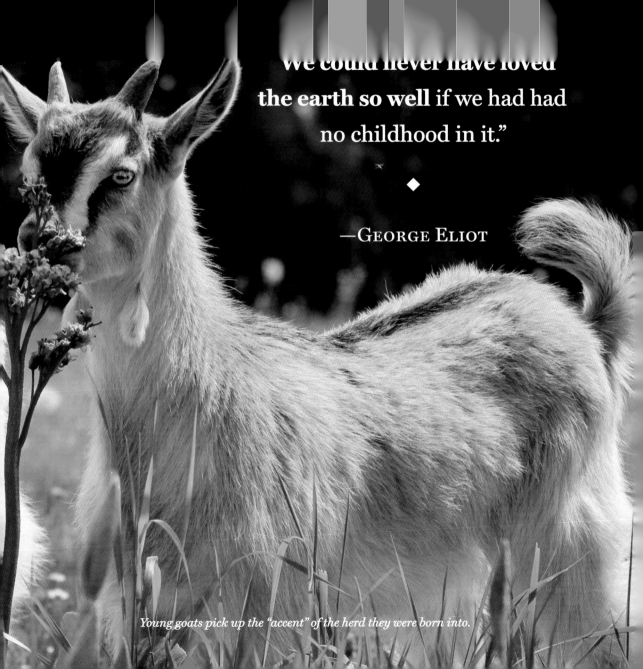

We could never have loved
the earth so well if we had had
no childhood in it."

◆

—GEORGE ELIOT

Young goats pick up the "accent" of the herd they were born into.

"Give a little love to a child,
and you get **a great deal back.**"

◆

—JOHN RUSKIN

*A kitten is born with hypersensitive whiskers
that help it navigate in the dark.*

Follow My Lead

After spending the first three months of their lives in the den, red fox kits are ready for adventure. The past few weeks have been busy, with the kits exploring around the den entrance, tumbling and tussling with each other, all under the watchful eyes of their mom and dad. Now they are bigger and know it's time to follow Dad's lead and learn to forage for themselves. Hunting is a particularly difficult task for the short-legged kits, lacking stealth and speed, but Dad will make sure they are prepared. He'll often bury prey near the den, then lead the kits on a pantomimed hunt as a way to demonstrate tracking scent. Dad also joins in his children's games, playing rough-house so they develop a hunter's strength. He knows that even when you're giving a lesson, you have to make time for fun.

There may be as many as 13 kits in one fox litter,
although five kits is the average.

Male swans are fearsome protectors of their families. The father is willing to face off with predators, competing birds, or even humans who get too close.

Monogamous swan couples live with their offspring for six to nine months, unusually long for waterfowl.

"I have found the **best way to give advice to your children** is to find out what they want and then advise them to do it."

◆

—HARRY S. TRUMAN

Hedgehogs whistle and twitter when they're upset, squeal when excited, and make content piglike grunts while foraging.

Have Baby, Will Socialize

Barbary macaques are like a lot of other monkeys—they are very social, and Mom takes on a lot of the child rearing with help from Dad. Dads are known to protect their offspring and will tend to their baby if it cries. But what makes Barbary macaque behavior unique is the close relationship between a male's social status and his child-rearing abilities. Dad has an extra incentive to help out with the little one: impressing his friends. Male Barbary macaques are known to use their children almost like an entry ticket to a certain clique of other macaques and to emphasize their place in the social hierarchy of the troop. Having a baby on their back increases their clout in the group. Plus, it makes for some good bonding time with their baby.

A male Barbary macaque will often place a baby between himself and another male in order to bond over grooming.

Male and female golden jackals hunt
as a team. They swallow prey whole,
then bring it back to the den as
a meal for their pups.

Young golden jackals usually stay with their parents for one year
after reaching maturity, helping to raise the next litter of pups.

"Enjoy the little things, for one day you may look back and realize they were the big things."

◆

—ROBERT BRAULT

A male Japanese puffer fish spends nine days drawing intricate sand patterns on the ocean floor. The female deposits her eggs in the center, where the water current is subdued.

Male Bonding

Newborn elephants are welcomed into a family group led by a strong matriarch. Female elephants will stay with that group, but when a young male grows older he begins to venture out on his own, away from the strongly bonded maternal family group that he was once a part of. Adolescent independence has its thrills, but it's also a period of transition. Luckily, roving bands of adult males often take in teenagers and help them learn the ropes, such as finding their place in the new social ranking. Even if none of the males in this adoptive group is the young elephant's father, they certainly become strong male role models. The friendships formed are often lifelong bonds.

Elephants have a longer pregnancy than any other mammal—almost 22 months.

"Time ripens all things.
No man is born wise."

◆

—MIGUEL DE CERVANTES SAAVEDRA

*Tigers have partially webbed toes and
are excellent swimmers as well as tree climbers.*

"Allow children to be **happy in their own way,** for what better way will they ever find?"

◆

—SAMUEL JOHNSON

Black bear cubs are born blind, tiny, and furless in their mother's winter den; but they may weigh 10 pounds (45 kg) by spring.

Leader of the Pack

From the moment they are born, wolf pups learn the importance of family and the pack. When new pups make their debut, all members of the pack pitch in to help, but of course, Mom and Dad give the most care and attention to the little ones. While Dad is guarding the den, Mom stays with the pups and nurses them for the first three weeks. When they get older, Dad and other adult wolves will help bring solid food to the pups, often regurgitating it for them. Dad also takes on the role of teacher when he begins to play with the pups, lead them on short hunts, and introduce them to the tight-knit pack. By springtime a chorus of high-pitched voices can be heard joining Dad's deep howl.

Wolf packs are established according to a strict hierarchy,
with a dominant male at the top and his mate not far behind.

Pandas that are free to choose their romantic partners are much more successful at mating and have more cubs than those paired by breeders.

Captive breeding of wild pandas is difficult, so the best way to ensure panda survival is by preserving their native habitat.

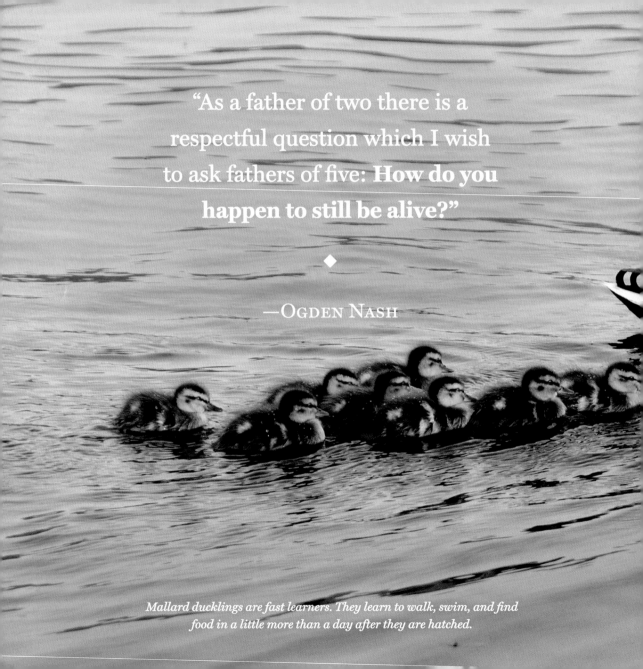

"As a father of two there is a respectful question which I wish to ask fathers of five: **How do you happen to still be alive?**"

◆

—OGDEN NASH

Mallard ducklings are fast learners. They learn to walk, swim, and find food in a little more than a day after they are hatched.

Precious Cargo

Seahorses are some of the most iconic marine life, with the face of a horse and a body like a mermaid. These upright swimming fish are found in shallow tropical waters around the world. The role of a seahorse father is unlike that of any other animal in the animal kingdom. Seahorses mate for life, but it is the father that becomes "pregnant." Seahorse fathers will carry the eggs in a special brood pouch for up to four weeks before giving birth. Depending on the species of seahorse, there can be as many as 1,500 eggs in one pregnancy. Dad keeps them safe as eggs, but baby seahorses, or fry, are independent from birth and learn to navigate their ocean environment on their own.

Seahorses anchor themselves with their prehensile tails to sea grasses and corals; then they use their elongated snouts to suck in plankton and small crustaceans that drift by.

If you see an night monkey in the wild carrying a baby, it's almost guaranteed to be the father. The children return to the mothers only for nursing.

Night monkeys are the only wild primates that are completely faithful to their partners. They stay with their mates for life and raise their own children.

"Nobody has ever measured,
even poets, **how much a heart
can hold."**

◆

—Zelda Fitzgerald

*When faced with a threat in the wild, an alpha stallion signals his family
to flee and leads them to safety. He will attack the intruder if necessary.*

Father to the Flock

Growing up in the desert of South Africa can be fraught with challenges, but luckily Namaqua sandgrouse chicks have their dad to help them. Within hours of their birth, Dad will lead the chicks to a food source, teaching them how to eat seeds from the ground. But finding water is not as easy. To help the chicks survive in the searing heat, Dad flies daily for the first two months of the chicks' lives to a water hole. Here he dips his belly feathers, which double as a water cooler, allowing him to travel long distances with life-giving water. For 15 minutes he rocks back and forth in the water to let his feathers soak up approximately two tablespoons of water like a sponge before returning to the nest. Once he arrives, his chicks use their beaks to drink the water from his feathers.

A Namaqua sandgrouse clutch typically has three eggs.

Wild dogs hunt as a pack but feed the pups first.

"Having one child **makes you a parent;**
having two you are a referee."

◆

—DAVID FROST

"**Have a heart that never hardens,**
and a temper that never tires,
and a touch that never hurts."

◆

—CHARLES DICKENS

*A male great horned owl not only selects the most suitable nest site
but also provides all sustenance for his family during the incubation
and brooding period.*

Piggyback Pop

The tropical rain forests of Papua New Guinea are known for their immense biodiversity of flora and fauna. It's here that certain species of frog fathers from the family Microhylidae care for their young. These frogs are unique in a few ways. Not only do they skip the tadpole stage, but the fathers are known to be the primary caregivers. The female departs quickly after laying the eggs, so it is up to Dad to guard the clutch. He protects the eggs from predators and keeps them hydrated until they are ready to hatch into tiny froglets. In many microhylid species, all the young—as many as 25—quickly climb upon Dad's back. He then embarks on a week-plus journey, moving 50 or so feet at a time and only at night. As he moves, the froglets jump off Dad's back, ready to begin life on their own in the rain forest.

A male Oreophryne *frog embraces his eggs as they begin to hatch into froglets.*

Gorilla patriarchs groom and cuddle their children, comfort them in times of distress, and act as disciplinarians during sibling squabbles.

Adult gorillas prefer to stay grounded, but juveniles love playing in trees, chasing one another and swinging from branch to branch.

"**Before I got married** I had six theories about bringing up children; now, I have six children and no theories."

◆

—JOHN WILMOT

The male rhea is a single parent. The mother has many mates,
but the father incubates the eggs and raises all the chicks as his own.

Travels With Dad

Wolverines are mysterious creatures that live in isolated areas throughout Alaska, Canada, Siberia, and parts of northern Europe. Wolverines can cover a lot of ground—they often have territories as big as those of grizzly bears, even though they are much smaller animals. However, wolverine fathers will forsake their preferred solitary lifestyle to foster a relationship with their young. This scenario is unique among solitary carnivores. While mothers do most of the child rearing, male wolverines are known to keep tabs on the kits by visiting the den every few days. Once the kits are old enough to venture out on their own, Dad doesn't give up on them. Wolverine males are known to meet up with their young and travel with them for a few days at a time.

The wolverine is the largest land-dwelling member of the weasel family.

Orca pods know it takes a village to raise a child. Adult males share in parenting whether the calves are their offspring, their siblings, or the offspring of another.

Orcas' community-centered approach to child rearing is called alloparenting.

"One thing I had learned from watching chimpanzees with their infants is that **having a child should be fun.**"

◆

—JANE GOODALL

Chimpanzees use facial expressions and body language including hand clapping, grooming, and kissing to communicate.

Your Biggest Fan

While dads are always supportive of their kids, the stickleback fish takes the role of a fan literally. Stickleback fish are found in temperate waters throughout the Northern Hemisphere. A male stickleback fish will build a marine nest for a female to lay eggs, sometimes as many as 200 at a time, and then becomes its sole guardian. While standing watch he also fans the eggs with his powerful pectoral fins to provide the eggs with necessary oxygen and keep the waters around the nest waste free. Once the eggs hatch, Dad's job still isn't done. He continues to protect the fry and teaches them the basics of self-defense by chasing them as if he were a predator, preparing them for life beyond the protected nest.

Stickleback fish can be found in freshwater and seawater.

"The best way to keep children home is to make the home atmosphere pleasant—**and let the air out of the tires.**"

◆

—Dorothy Parker

The male flamingo nests with his monogamous partner, helps incubate eggs, and produces nutrient-rich "crop milk" to feed his babies.

"We find delight in the **beauty and happiness of children** that makes the heart too big for the body."

◆

—RALPH WALDO EMERSON

Pigs are among the smartest of all domesticated animals.
Their intelligence can match or even surpass that of dogs.

Illustrations Credits

Beavers form close-knit families, with attentive fathers. The children live up to two years in the lodge built by their monogamous parents.

For *the* Amazing Mom *in* Your Life

Filled with countless adorable animals and heartfelt celebrations of motherhood, this book is a charming keepsake for every mom.

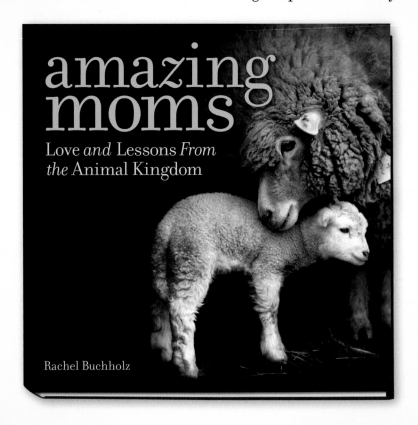